Famous Leaders

by Andrew Langley

a Capstone company — publishers for children

Engage Literacy is published in the UK by Raintree.
Raintree is an imprint of Capstone Global Library Limited, a company incorporated in England and Wales having its registered office at 264 Banbury Road, Oxford, OX2 7DY – Registered company number: 6695582

www.raintree.co.uk

Editorial Credits
Editor: Alesha Sullivan
Designer: Peggie Carley and Cynthia Della-Rovere
Media Researcher: Kelly Garvin
Production Specialist: Steve Walker

Image credits
Getty Images: Dinodia Photos, cover (bottom right), Print Collector, 10, Stock Montage, 7, 23, The Print Collector Heritage Images, 19, Universal History Archive, 33, William Lovelace/Stringer, 34; Newscom: akg-images, backcover, 12, 29, 51, Album/Prisma, cover (top right), Album/sfgp, 45, 58, Balkis Press/ ABACA, 36-37, I.D.A.F/SIPA, 55, Ingram Publishing, 46, Pictures From History, 24, Sovfoto Universal Images Group, 49 (bottom), Stapleton Historical Collection Heritage Images, 30, World History Archive, 35, 57; Shutterstock: 360b, 61, Andrey Burmakin, 63, Eder, 1, Everett-Art, 15, 20, 39, Everett Historical, 27, 31,40, 43, ixpert, cover (top left), Morphart Creation, 17, Nikonaft, 5, Peter Hermes Furian, 8-9, 13, 49 (top), Sergio TB, cover (bottom left), Triff, cover (background), 53

Artistic elements: Shutter: Arcady, GraphicStore, maglyvi, siro46, Triff

21 20 19
10 9 8 7 6 5 4 3 2 1
Printed and bound in India.

Famous Leaders

ISBN: 978 1 4747 4589 5

Contents

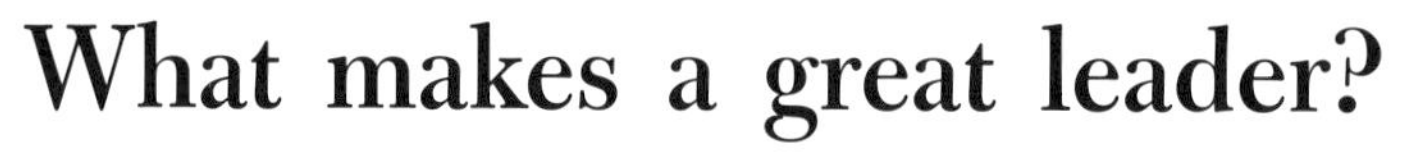

What makes a great leader?

There are many leaders in the world. Every nation has a leader. So does every city, sports team and school. But what makes a great leader?

The greatest leaders in history had many impressive qualities. They have had strong goals and motivation. Some, like Napoleon Bonaparte, wanted to make their countries powerful. Some, such as Queen Elizabeth I and Franklin D Roosevelt, wanted to defeat an unsafe enemy. Some, such as Nelson Mandela, wanted to fight for freedom. Famous leaders have changed the course of history around the world.

This statue of French leader Napoleon Bonaparte is located in Paris.

Empire builders

Alexander the Great (356–323 BC)

Around 2,300 years ago, Alexander was a prince and soldier in ancient Greece who had one aim – to conquer the whole world. His father, King Philip II, was ruler of Macedonia, a kingdom in what is now northern Greece. Alexander learned to be a soldier. He fought his first battle when he was only 16 years old. But in 336 BC enemies murdered his father. Alexander became the new king of Macedonia.

Alexander quickly showed he was a strong leader. His armies took control of the rest of Greece. Then in 334 BC, he led them overseas into Asia. When the crew landed, Alexander jabbed his spear into the soil. It was a challenge. He was going to conquer the mighty empire of Persia, which was located where the country of Iran is today.

Fact

"BC" is short for "Before Christ". This means all of history before Jesus was born. Jesus was the founder of the Christian religion.

Alexander the Great

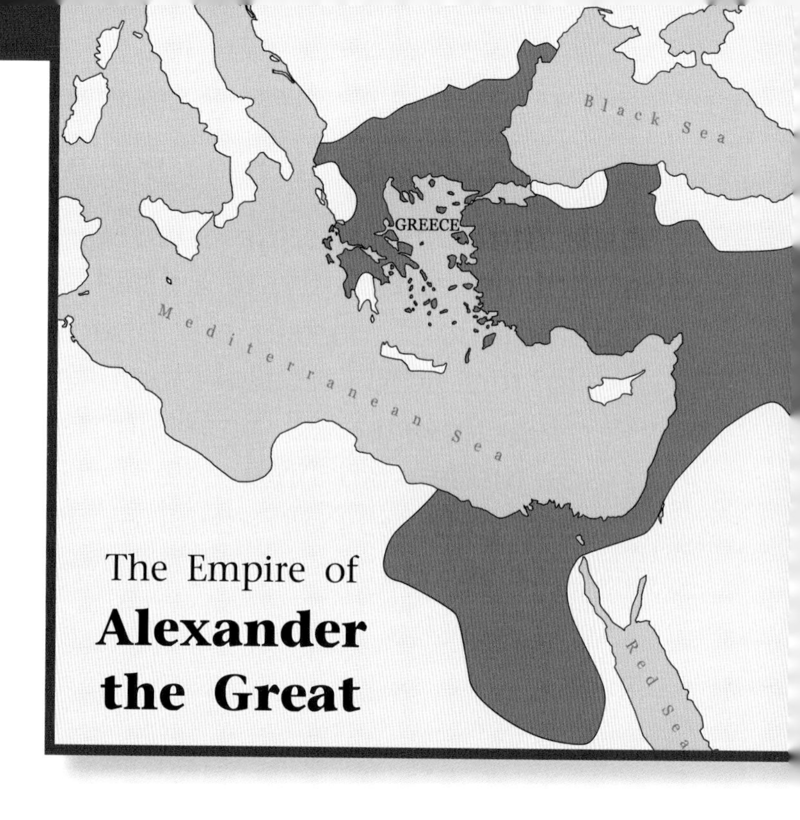

Alexander and his army moved across Persia within a year and with great success. He was an excellent leader, and his troops never lost a battle. Their successes took them to regions now covered by Turkey, Syria, Iraq and Egypt.

By 331 BC, Alexander was the Great King of Persia and the *pharaoh* of Egypt. But he wanted more. He marched towards the east. The Macedonian army climbed up into the high mountains of Afghanistan, then down into the plains of India.

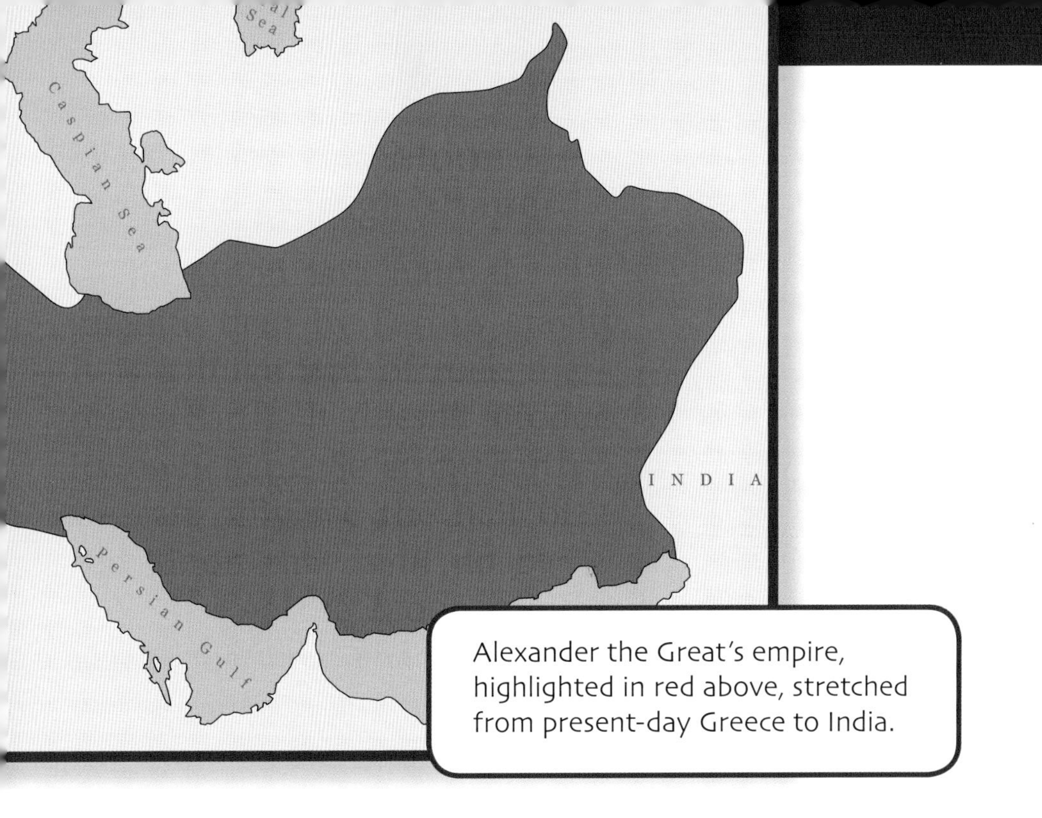

Alexander the Great's empire, highlighted in red above, stretched from present-day Greece to India.

When the army was in India, the men stopped and refused to carry on. They had been away from Greece for nine years. Alexander agreed to start the long journey home, but he never made it. He died in 323 BC in the city of Babylon in present-day Iraq. Alexander's empire covered more than a million square kilometres at the time of his death.

Julius Caesar (100–44 BC)

About 2,100 years ago, Julius Caesar was born into a wealthy family in 100 BC in ancient Rome, Italy. He quickly grew powerful as a soldier and a *statesman*, which is a member of the government. In 59 BC, against the opinion of the Senate, Caesar was elected as a consul, one of the city's major leaders. A year later, he was named governor of Gaul. He was now in charge of a huge area, covering modern France, Belgium and northern Italy.

Julius Caesar led his men to many victories for the Roman Empire.

By 49 BC Caesar and his men had won many triumphs across the region. The Roman Empire was now the strongest reign, or period of rule, in the world. But it was time to come home. Caesar knew he would have to face bitter enemies in Rome. He led his troops back into Italy. A civil war broke out between the Republic of Italy's army and Caesar's troops. After a year Caesar took complete control of Rome.

Many Romans wanted Caesar to become the king of the empire. But his enemies did not agree. On 15 March 44 BC, Caesar's rivals stabbed him to death at the Senate meeting house. Julius Caesar is known for strengthening the Roman government and his surrounding empire. He will always be known as a brave and bold leader.

"Veni, Vidi, Vici – I came, I saw, I conquered."

Caesar had these words painted on one of his wagons after his swift *invasion* of the Pontus region, in what is now Turkey.

Genghis Khan (c.1162–1227)

Mongol leader Temujin, later known as Genghis Khan, built an empire in present-day central Asia and China in the early 1200s. His *conquests* helped to open up the Silk Road, a trade route between Europe and China. But he started with almost nothing. He was born circa (c.), or around, 1162 and grew up in the grasslands of Mongolia. *Nomadic* tribes throughout the grasslands moved from place to place and fought each other for land and food.

Temujin was a born leader. As he grew older, he gathered a band of followers. They became an army, which Temujin used to defeat local tribes in order to gain control of their lands. Historians believe that in 1189, there was a group of Temujin's supporters at Blue Lake in Mongolia. They shouted that Temujin was "Genghis Khan" – the "Ruler of All!"

Genghis Khan, born Temujin, was the founder of the Mongol Empire.

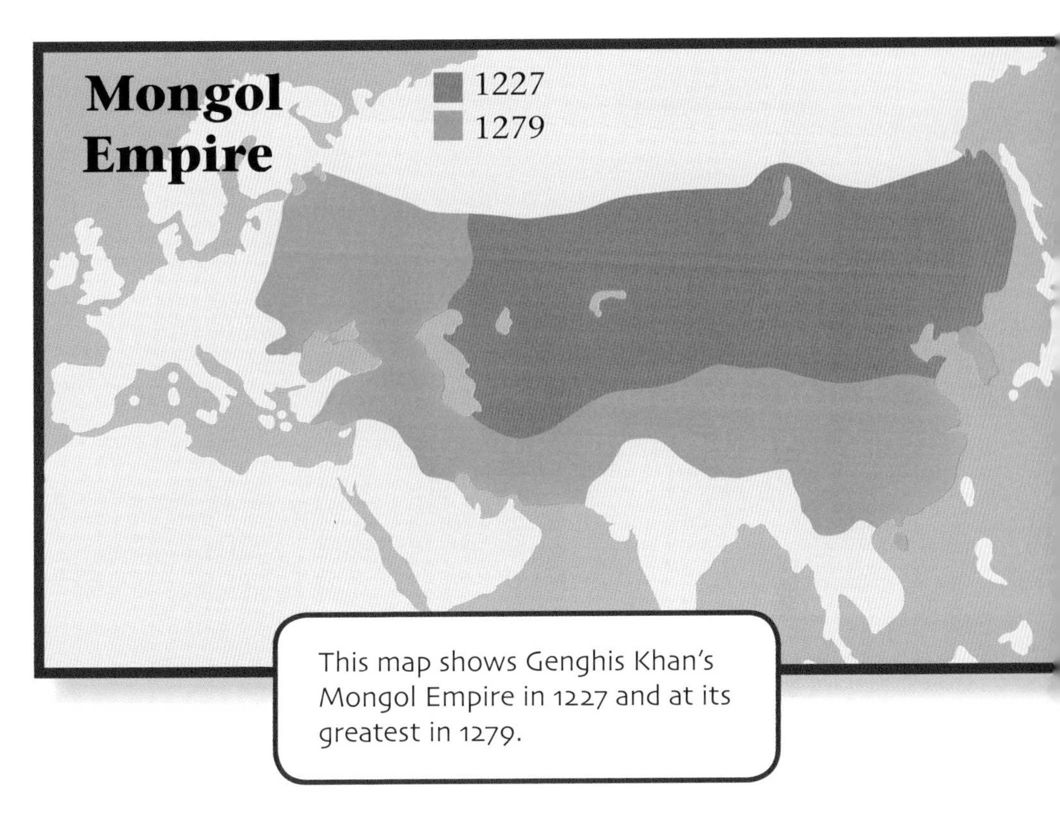

This map shows Genghis Khan's Mongol Empire in 1227 and at its greatest in 1279.

Temujin set out to make himself even more powerful. The Mongol armies swept through China and captured Beijing. Then they turned west, into Afghanistan and what was then Persia. By the time Temujin died in 1227, his empire stretched from the Black Sea to the shores of Japan. Genghis Khan helped set up free trade in Mongolia, so traders were able to travel safely along the Silk Road carrying goods, such as spices and silk.

Napoleon Bonaparte (1769–1821)

Napoleon Bonaparte was an important leader of change in Europe. He was born in 1769 on the French island of Corsica and trained as a soldier in France. He later became a military leader and a key ruler of France.

During the French Revolution (1789–1799), rebels overthrew the king of France. Napoleon soon became a general in the army. He won a string of wins in Italy and later conquered Egypt in 1798, claiming control for France. Soon France was one of the strongest nations in Europe.

A year later Napoleon returned to France and took power. Napoleon improved the country's laws and tax system, such as collecting taxes from the people. He also ordered the country's roads and bridges to be improved. In 1804 Napoleon crowned himself emperor of France.

Napoleon Bonaparte

Many nearby countries were alarmed by Napoleon's new status. They realized that he wanted to make France larger and stronger by invading its neighbours. In 1805 Napoleon won the greatest of his triumphs. His troops beat the Russians and Austrians at the Battle of Austerlitz, called the Battle of the Three Emperors.

The French conquered large parts of Europe. In 1812 Napoleon planned to invade Russia. The Russians outsmarted Napoleon by retreating, or pulling back, whenever Napoleon's troops tried to attack. Soon Napoleon moved too deep into Russia, running low on supplies. He had to flee. In 1814 Napoleon was forced to surrender and was sent to live on the Italian island of Elba.

Napoleon did not give up. In 1815 he escaped from Elba and sailed to France. Cheering crowds in Paris welcomed him. But he was not free for long. Later that year, Napoleon's forces were beaten in Waterloo, Belgium, by the British and Prussian armies. This time the enemies sent Napoleon to live on the remote Atlantic island of St Helena, where he died in 1821.

Waterloo facts and figures			
	Infantry (soldiers on foot)	Cavalry (soldiers on horse)	Deaths
French	48,950	15,760	25,000
British and Prussian	49,600	12,400	23,000

This illustration shows Napoleon's return to France in 1815.

Female rulers

Hatshepsut (c.1507–1458 BC)

Pharaohs ruled ancient Egypt for more than 3,000 years. Many people think they were all men, but it is believed that at least seven were women. One of the first and most powerful female rulers was Hatshepsut.

Hatshepsut was a royal princess. She was married to Tuthmose II, who became pharaoh. When Tuthmose II died in 1479 BC, nearly 3,500 years ago, his only child was a baby. The boy was too young to run a great empire. Hatshepsut took over as ruler until he was old enough.

But Hatshepsut had bigger plans. She crowned herself pharaoh of Egypt. Hatshepsut was the first documented female ruler of Egypt in history. She felt she had the right to rule Egypt. Her reign lasted over 20 years. During her time in command, Egypt had the world's largest army. When Hatshepsut died, she was buried in the Valley of the Kings next to other powerful pharaohs.

Fact

Hatshepsut wore the same striped head cloth as male kings. She also wore a false beard!

Queen Elizabeth I

Elizabeth I (1533–1603)

Elizabeth was the daughter of England's King Henry VIII and Queen Anne Boleyn. However, it seemed unlikely that Elizabeth would ever have the opportunity to be queen. Men had always ruled England. Her brother, Edward, was next in line to be king.

King Henry VIII died in 1547, and Edward took over the throne. Edward died a few years later. Edward and Elizabeth's sister, Mary, was crowned Queen of England. Mary was a strong believer in the Catholic faith and feared Elizabeth, who believed in the Protestant faith, would try and take the throne. For a time, she imprisoned Elizabeth in the Tower of London.

Mary's reign only lasted for five years before she also died. Elizabeth became Queen of England in 1558. Clashes between Catholics and Protestants swept through England. One of Elizabeth's first acts was to make England a Protestant country again, as it was when her father, King Henry VIII, ruled.

Queen Elizabeth I instantly began improving her government and handing out announcements called *proclamations*. She wanted to ease tensions between France and England. The queen faced many dangers during her reign. The biggest threat came from the kings of France and Spain. They backed plots to kill the queen and to place her cousin Mary, Queen of Scots, on the throne. These plots all failed.

In 1587 Elizabeth declared that Mary, Queen of Scots, was aiding the enemy and was a *traitor* to England. Elizabeth ordered her death. The Spanish took revenge by sending a great fleet to invade England the following year. The English navy drove the attacking ships away. A fierce storm destroyed at least half of the fleet.

Queen Elizabeth I was one of the greatest and most popular of all British rulers. In her reign, England grew wealthy and powerful. She died on 24 March 1603.

Queen Elizabeth I

Queen Nzinga ruled in Matamba from 1631 until her death in 1663.

Nzinga of Ndongo (c.1583–1663)

Ana de Sousa Nzinga Mbande was born a princess. Her family ruled the Ndongo region in Angola, West Africa. At the time, the Portuguese had invaded the West African coast. They came to take Africans and force them into slavery in North America.

Nzinga's brother, Ngola Mbande, became king of Ndongo in 1617. He tried to make peace with the Portuguese. In 1622 they held a peace meeting. The king did not want to go, so he sent Nzinga instead. Nzinga proved to be a good *diplomat,* or representative for her people. She helped put peace treaties, also called agreements, into place, but they did not last.

Nzinga came to power after the death of her brother in 1624. The Portuguese troops ordered Queen Nzinga to force the Ndongo people into slavery. Queen Nzinga refused and began a long war against the Portuguese, sending her troops into many battles. She did not succeed in driving out the invaders. However, Nzinga is remembered today as a heroic fighter for Ndongo's freedom.

Catherine the Great (1729–1796)

Brave and clever, Catherine the Great grew up to be one of the most famous and longest-ruling female leaders in Russian history. Born Sophie Friederike Auguste von Anhalt-Zerbst, Catherine was the daughter of a Prussian prince. At the age of 15, she was sent against her will to Russia to marry Prince Peter III.

Catherine's husband, Peter III, was made tsar, or ruler, of Russia in 1762. Russia was at war with Prussia. Catherine soon learned that her husband was weak and not able to rule the vast Russian Empire. Helped by the palace guards, Catherine forced her husband to give up the throne. She was crowned empress of Russia in his place.

During her long reign, Catherine set out to make Russia richer and stronger. She told farmers to grow more food and opened silver mines and factories. She built more schools, many of which were for girls. The Russian Empire grew larger, as her armies invaded Poland, Ukraine and Georgia. Catherine died in 1796, after ruling for more than 30 years.

Fact

The empress was very good at copying animal noises. She loved giving "concerts", where she would growl, purr and spit like a cat.

Fighting for rights

Chief Sitting Bull (c.1831–1890)

Tatanka Iyotake, better known as Sitting Bull, was born in the Black Hills of South Dakota, USA. He belonged to the Sioux nation, a group of Native Americans who had lived and hunted there for many years. Sitting Bull grew up to be a brave and skillful leader during a period when the American nation was rapidly growing. He was named head chief of the Lakota Sioux in 1868.

Sitting Bull's home and native land was in danger. White settlers from the eastern United States began moving into South Dakota. In the 1870s, the US government wanted to purchase the Black Hills from the Sioux Nation. But Chief Sitting Bull refused. He helped unite the Sioux Nation to defend their native land.

In 1876 the US government sent soldiers to invade the Black Hills. Sitting Bull was one of the chiefs who led the Sioux in battle against General George Custer's soldiers at the Battle of Little Bighorn. The defeat was Sitting Bull's last major win. More US troops came to the Black Hills to take revenge against the Sioux, and Sitting Bull fled to Canada with his people.

Chief Sitting Bull returned to South Dakota in 1881, where he was held prisoner for two years. He was later shot and killed by a policeman in 1890 outside his cabin. Throughout his life, Chief Sitting Bull honoured his people's way of living and fought to protect the Sioux's homeland.

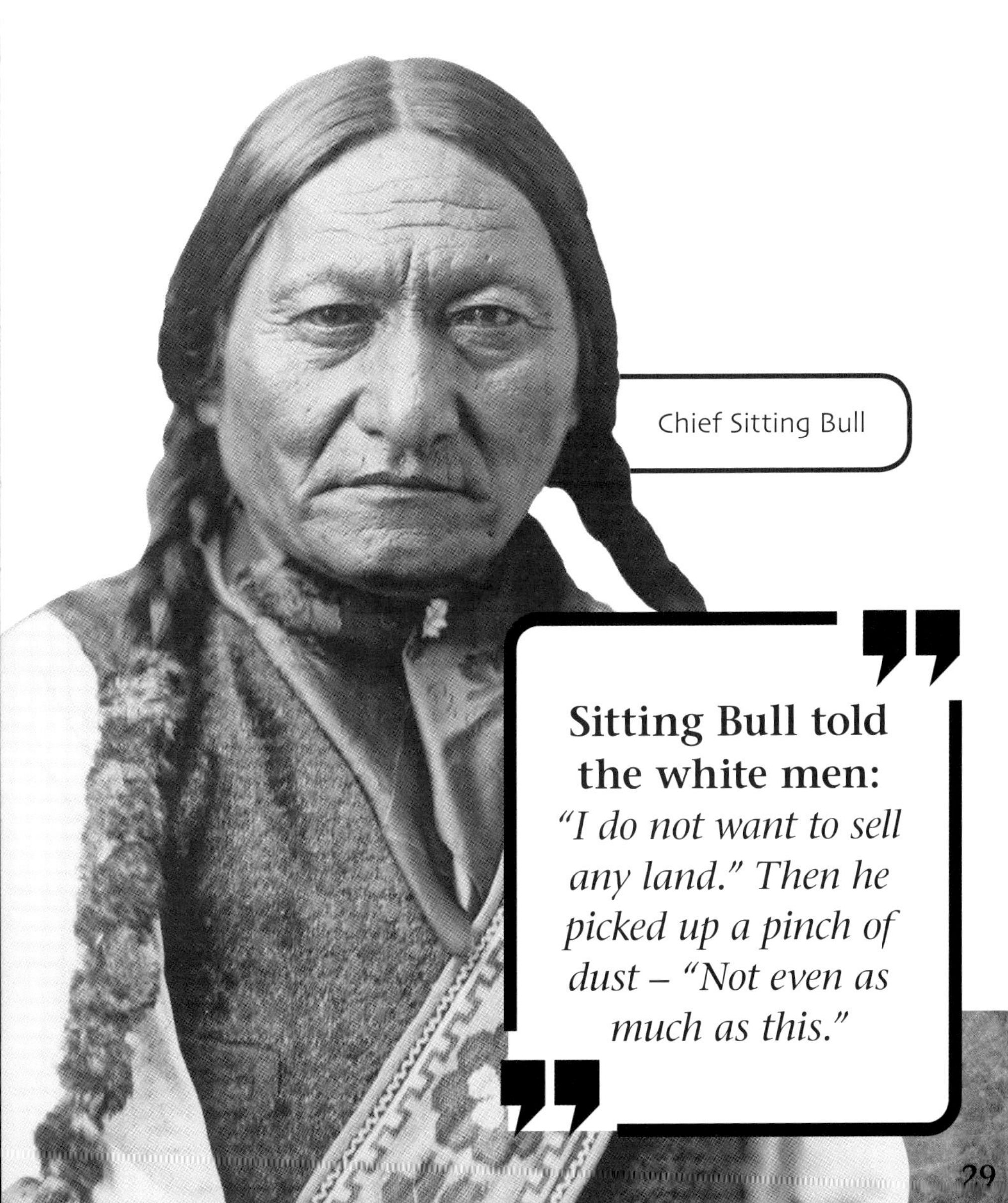

Chief Sitting Bull

Sitting Bull told the white men: *"I do not want to sell any land." Then he picked up a pinch of dust – "Not even as much as this."*

Emmeline Pankhurst (1858–1928)

Emmeline Pankhurst was a women's rights *activist* in Great Britain. Many female activists were pushing for equal rights. In the mid-1800s, women could not vote in elections. Pankhurst married in 1879, and with her husband, she led a movement for women's *suffrage,* or right to vote. In 1903 she helped create the Women's Social and Political Union (WSPU). The WSPU's goal was to achieve women's right to vote.

At first, few people took notice of the WSPU's movement. Then in 1907 its members started taking violent action. They threw stones through windows and set fire to government buildings. Pankhurst and others were sent to prison. When they refused to eat, they were fed by force.

This photo shows Emmeline Pankhurst in her prison cell.

Pankhurst and her "suffragettes", as they were called, kept fighting until 1928. That year the law was changed so that women had the same voting rights as men. Pankhurst died a few months later. For many people, Pankhurst represents the pained yet successful efforts of women's suffrage.

Susan B. Anthony

Born in 1820, Susan B. Anthony fought for women's rights in the United States. She travelled around the country forming gatherings and giving speeches. Anthony faced many challenges while fighting for women's voting rights, equal wages for women and the right for women to own property. In 1920 American women finally won the right to vote, 14 years after Anthony's death.

Dr Martin Luther King Jr (1929–1968)

Dr Martin Luther King Jr was born in Atlanta, Georgia, in the USA. He became a Baptist minister, just like his father. At this time, African-Americans did not have the same rights as white Americans. King's faith motivated him to lead a movement to acquire legal equality and fair rights for African-Americans in the United States.

King led many peaceful protests for members of his race. King used the power of words to help achieve his goals. King helped arrange a March on Washington, demanding jobs and equal rights for African-Americans. He wanted to end the separation of white and black schools, among many other things. In 1963 more than 250,000 people gathered at the Lincoln Memorial in Washington, DC, where King gave a speech entitled "I Have a Dream". The speech called for friendship and unity among all Americans, no matter their skin colour.

"I have a dream that one day this nation will rise up and live out the true meaning of its creed: 'We hold these truths to be self-evident, that all men are created equal.'"

This photo was taken during Dr Martin Luther King Jr's "I Have a Dream" speech.

A year later, the US Congress passed the Civil Rights Act. The Civil Rights Act outlawed *discrimination.* It also outlawed unfair treatment based on gender or national origin. In 1965 the Voting Rights Act was passed, outlawing racial discrimination at the polls. Martin Luther King Jr was a champion of justice. At the age of 35, he won the Nobel Peace Prize for being a leader of social change. Four years later, King was shot dead in Memphis, Tennessee.

This photo shows Dr Martin Luther King Jr and his wife, Coretta Scott King, leading a black voting rights march from Selma, Alabama, to the state capital in Montgomery.

Rosa Parks

Rosa Parks

In 1955 Rosa Parks made history in Montgomery, Alabama. After a long day of work, Parks was sitting in the "coloured" section on a bus on her way home. Soon the section for whites was full, and white passengers were standing. The driver told Parks to leave her seat so the white people could sit down. She refused and was arrested. Parks' action sparked protests against the unfair treatment of black people. Nearly a year later, the Montgomery bus system stopped forcing the separation of blacks and whites on its buses.

Malala Yousafzai (1997)

Malala Yousafzai was born in north-west Pakistan. Her father ran a school near the family's home. He knew it was important for Pakistani boys and girls to have an education. Malala loved being at school.

By 2009 their town was under the control of the extreme political movement known as the Taliban. The Taliban enforced a strict version of Islamic laws, including not allowing girls to go to school. But that didn't stop Malala. She challenged the Taliban by attending classes and began writing a blog for the British Broadcasting Corporation. Malala wrote about life under Taliban rule and how she was afraid the Taliban would attack her school.

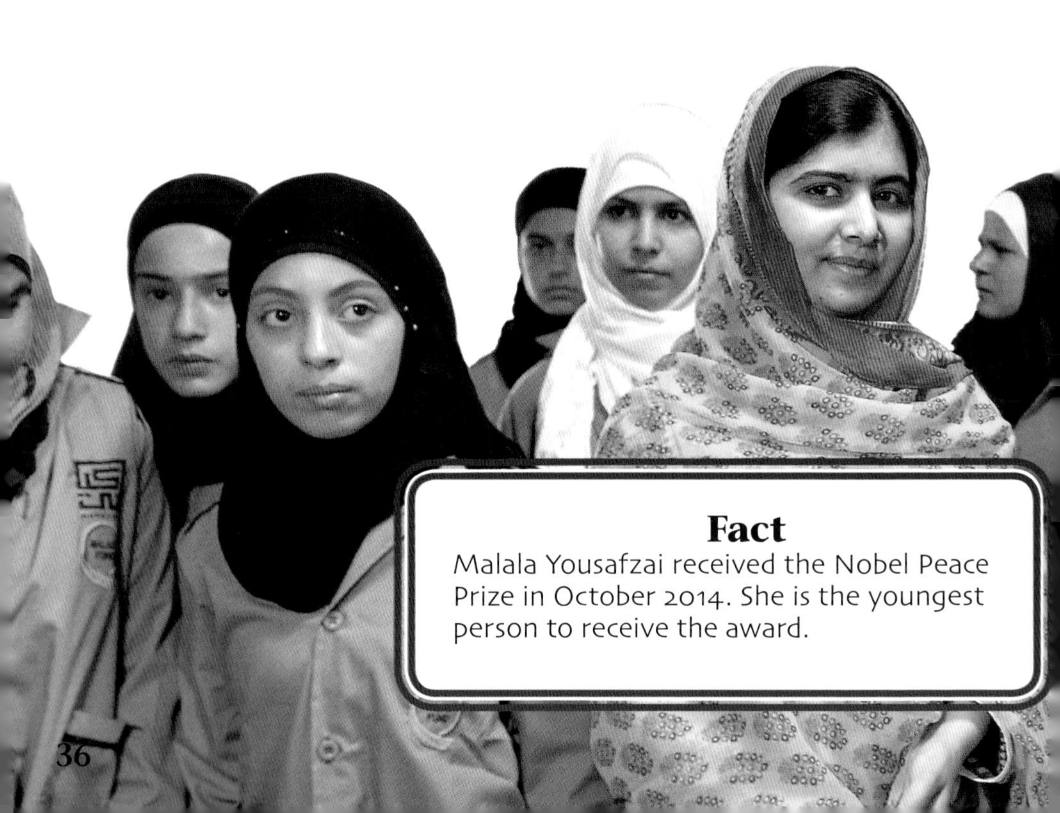

Fact

Malala Yousafzai received the Nobel Peace Prize in October 2014. She is the youngest person to receive the award.

The Taliban hated Malala's blog. They threatened to kill her, but she and her father continued to speak out for the right to education. On 9 October 2012, Malala was on the bus going home from school. A member of the Taliban came onto the bus and shot her in the head. Malala nearly died. She was flown to Birmingham, in the UK, where she was treated and recovered in January 2013. Since then, Malala and her father created the Malala Fund. Through the Malala Fund, she has become a global activist for girls' education.

Malala Yousafzai, in yellow, is shown with women at the Malala Yousafzai All-Girls School in Lebanon in 2015.

Wartime leaders

George Washington (1732–1799)

George Washington was born in Virginia, USA, in 1732. At the time, Virginia was an American *colony* ruled by Great Britain. Settlers from Europe controlled most of the colonies. British forces were fighting France for the control of North America. In 1752 Washington joined the local army and later went into battle with British forces against the French.

In 1758 Washington left the army and returned to his home in Mount Vernon, Virginia. Washington was unhappy that a foreign country governed his homeland. Like many other Americans, he wanted the colonies to break away from British power. In 1775 a war broke out between the colonists and Britain. Washington was chosen to be the commander-in-chief of the American forces.

One of Washington's greatest successes was at Yorktown, Virginia, in 1781. Washington's troops helped win the war by forcing Britain to surrender. The American colonies broke their ties with Britain and became independent. Washington wanted to retire, but in 1789 he was chosen to be the first president of the United States. His strength and firmness saw his young nation through a challenging period.

George Washington

Abraham Lincoln

Abraham Lincoln (1809–1865)

Abraham Lincoln was born in a one-room log cabin in Kentucky, USA, on 12 February 1809. Growing up, Lincoln worked hard to help support his family. There was little time for formal schooling, but Lincoln read many books and taught himself.

At the age of 21, Lincoln moved to Illinois, where he took a number of jobs. He became involved in local politics and was soon elected to the Illinois state legislature, which is a group of people who make and change laws. In 1845 Lincoln ran for US Congress and served one term for two years.

During the 1850s, the biggest issue in Congress was slavery. The use of slaves was legal in southern states, though some people believed it should be allowed in other states. Lincoln and many others in the northern states argued that slavery should be *abolished,* or put to an end.

Fact

Abraham Lincoln became a self-taught lawyer in 1836.

In November 1860, Lincoln was elected the 16th president of the United States. Southern states feared Lincoln would take away the states' rights and end slavery. In the next few months, 11 southern states formed a new country called the Confederate States of America. In April 1861, a civil war started between the Confederates and the government, led by Lincoln.

Lincoln wanted to keep peace in the United States. The Civil War carried on for four years, and hundreds of thousands of Americans died. During the war, Lincoln made an order called the Emancipation Proclamation, which stated that all slaves in Confederate states were free.

Lincoln was elected president again in 1864. A year later the Confederates surrendered, and the Civil War ended. Lincoln promoted the healing and rebuilding of America. Less than one week later, Lincoln was shot at Ford's Theatre in Washington, DC, and died the next day.

CASUALTIES OF THE CIVIL WAR

	Union troops	Confederate troops
Total troops	1,566,678	1,082,119
Wounded	275,175	194,000*
Died of wounds	110,070	94,000
Died of disease	249,458	164,000

– Garraty and McCaughey, *The American Nation*, Harper and Row, 1987;
*Shelby Foote, *The Civil War: A Narrative*, Vintage Books, 1986

This painting shows Abraham Lincoln and the first reading of the Emancipation Proclamation in 1862.

Sir Winston Churchill (1874–1965)

Sir Winston Churchill spent most of his life in government. He was a leading British statesman for more than 40 years and devoted himself to public service, such as fighting for workers' rights and the improvement of the public health system. Churchill helped the British get through the most dangerous days of World War II (1939–1945).

In the late 1930s, Nazi power was growing throughout Europe under German leader Adolf Hitler. British leaders wanted to make peace with Hitler. But Churchill warned that the Nazis were a terrible threat. Churchill was right. In 1939 Great Britain and France declared war against Germany after Hitler's armies invaded nearby Poland. The next year, Churchill became the British prime minister and immediately set about drawing up Britain's wartime strategy.

Churchill's speeches pushed the British to keep fighting. He worked with the leaders of the United States, Soviet Union and France to form the Allied powers. The Allies were against Germany and the other Axis powers, Japan and Italy. By 1945 Hitler and the Nazi Party were conquered, ending World War II after nearly six years.

Fact

Winston Churchill was a Member of Parliament for 61 years – longer than anyone else.

Franklin Delano Roosevelt

Franklin D. Roosevelt (1882–1945)

Success came easily to Franklin Delano Roosevelt. He was born in 1882 into a wealthy New York family. Roosevelt ran for the New York Senate at the age of 28 and won. Roosevelt was efficient throughout his early political career, despite having been diagnosed with polio at the age of 39.

The Great Depression struck the United States in 1929. Banks and other businesses closed around the world, which sparked an economic disaster. Many people lost their jobs and their savings. Millions of Americans were unemployed or homeless. Roosevelt was elected the 32nd president of the United States in 1932. Americans widely respected him. Roosevelt helped create new jobs and created a banking system that protected people's money. Roosevelt was elected president again in 1936 and in 1940.

The country was thriving. In 1941 America entered World War II. US forces joined the Allies in the fight against Germany and the Axis countries. Roosevelt played a key role in beating Germany through a series of invasions. The Allies claimed victory in 1945. Roosevelt died of a stroke later that year.

Georgy Zhukov (1896–1974)

Georgy Zhukov was the most successful Soviet officer during World War II. Born into a poor family, he joined the Red Army of the Soviet Union in 1917. He rose to become an expert in tank warfare and a leader of the 1st Cavalry Army.

When World War II began in 1939, the Soviet Union was on Germany's side. However, in 1941 the Nazi German leader Adolf Hitler turned his back on his ally. Hitler attacked the Soviet Union, and the Russians declared war on Germany.

Zhukov was now the head of the Red Army. He took charge of the Russian city of Stalingrad, which was in danger of German capture. After one of the deadliest combats in history, the Germans were forced to surrender at the Battle of Stalingrad in 1943.

A year later, Zhukov led the Red Army to success over the Germans at the Battle of Kursk. The win was a turning point of the war. Zhukov's troops stormed into Germany and captured the capital, Berlin. Georgy Zhukov's brave leadership helped bring an end to World War II in Europe.

Georgy Zhukov

Shaping the modern world

Mahatma Gandhi (1869–1948)

Mahatma Gandhi was born in north-west India on 2 October 1869. Gandhi's childhood was filled with teachings of non-violence and the belief that everything in the universe is everlasting. Throughout his life, he was best known for his peaceful protests to fight for change without the use of violence.

In 1888 Gandhi sailed to London to study law. He also studied many religions, such as Hinduism, Buddhism and others. In 1893 Gandhi accepted a contract at a law firm in South Africa. However, Gandhi soon realized that many Africans were highly discriminated against by white South Africans. He started a movement for equal rights for all races.

Mahatma Gandhi

Gandhi faced the same problem when he returned home to India later in 1915. The British had ruled his country for many years. Gandhi spent the rest of his life fighting for Indian independence. He planned many peaceful protests. In 1922, he was put in prison for his involvement in the protests. Gandhi's fame spread, and his followers called him "Mahatma", meaning "Great Soul".

In 1930 Britain put a tax on salt. Gandhi led thousands of Indians on a 400-kilometre march to the sea, where they gathered salt for free. Again, Gandhi was imprisoned for disobeying the law. He now had many supporters. Soon the British were forced to discuss the laws with Gandhi. Over the following years, the government followed through with their promised agreements, including rights for women and efforts to lessen poverty in India.

Fact

As a boy, Gandhi was very shy. He would run home from school so he didn't have to talk to anyone.

At last, in 1947, India celebrated its independence from Britain. The country was split into two regions – India and Pakistan. Conflict quickly arose between the two countries. Gandhi saw the need for political parties to work together towards a common goal. He spent the next few months working towards Hindu–Muslim peace. He visited places where there were riots. On 30 January 1948, Mahatma Gandhi was shot and killed on his way to a prayer meeting in Delhi, India.

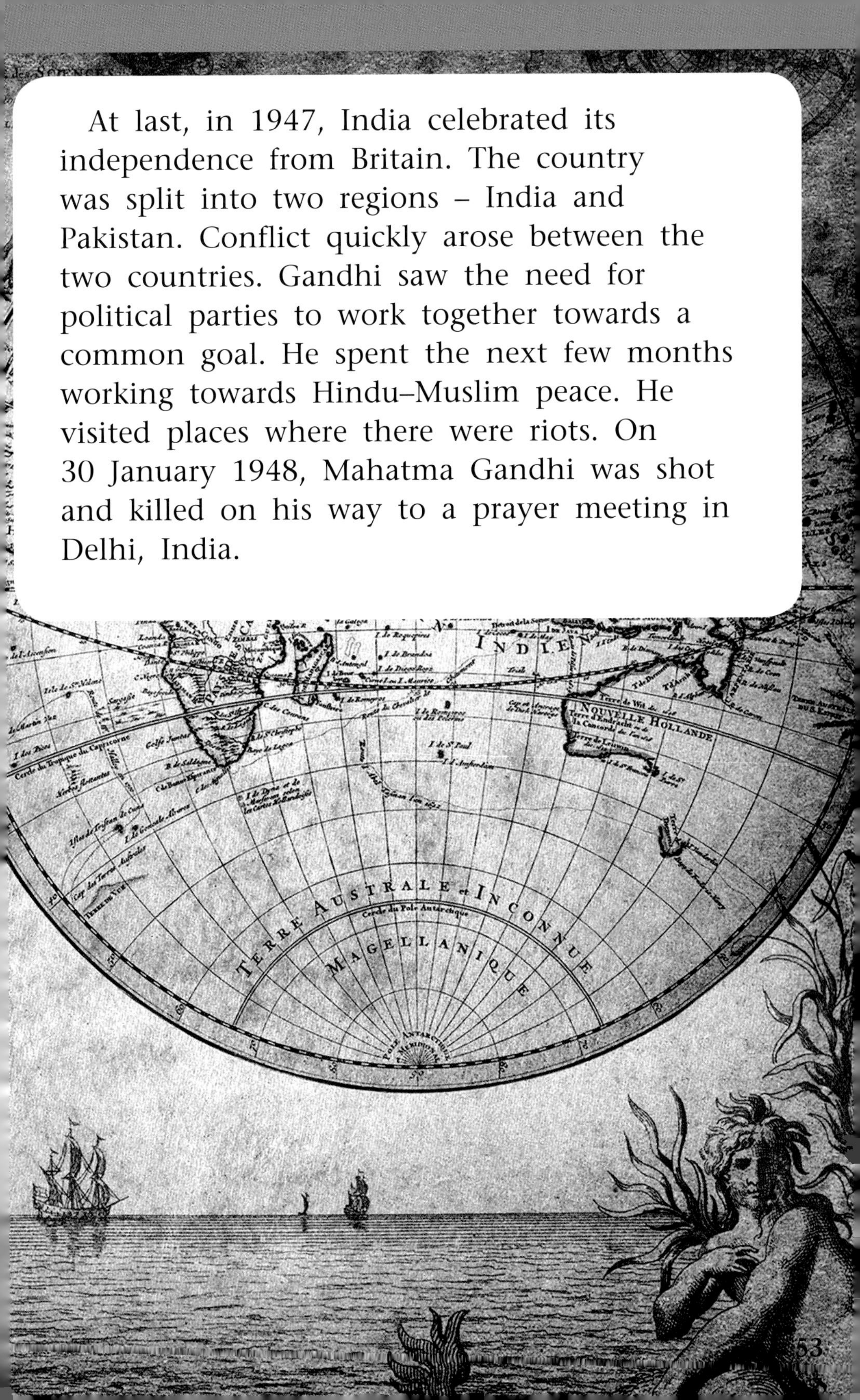

Nelson Mandela (1918–2013)

Nelson Mandela was born on 18 July 1918, in South Africa. He spent his childhood looking after his family's sheep and cattle. He would listen to his family's stories of wars and other struggles. From a young age, Mandela dreamed of being a part of the fight for freedom with his people.

British rulers had controlled South Africa for many years. Black people native to the country had few rights, and most lived in poverty. In 1948 the government started a system called "apartheid", which separated blacks and whites through the use of harsh laws.

Mandela joined the struggle for black freedom in the 1940s. He became a leading member of the African National Congress (ANC). For 20 years, Mandela led peaceful activism against the South African government without the use of violence. In 1956 Mandela and 150 other protestors were arrested and charged with *treason* for betraying his country. The charges were dropped five years later.

This photo shows Nelson Mandela in his earlier years.

In 1962 Nelson Mandela was arrested again. He and seven others were accused of plotting to attack the government. They were sentenced to life in prison. Mandela became famous around the world as a freedom fighter.

Many people did not agree with the South African government's system of racial discrimination. Mass protests took place all over the country. The apartheid government was forced to give in. In February 1990, Mandela was released from prison after 27 years. People cheered all over the world.

The first governmental elections where more than one race was allowed to run were held in 1994. Mandela became the first black president of South Africa at the age of 77. He retired after one five-year term and died in 2013. He will be remembered for helping to reform the South African government and as an *advocate* for human rights.

Nelson Mandela

Mikhail Gorbachev (1931)

Mikhail Gorbachev grew up on a farm in the Soviet Union, now known as Russia. He had a passion for learning. Gorbachev became a member of the Communist Party while he was in high school. The Communist Party believes all land, homes and businesses belong to the government. For many years, there had been conflict between the Soviet Union and the United States over their differing styles of government. This often prevented the two powerful nations from reaching agreements on key policy issues.

Mikhail Gorbachev

Gorbachev quickly rose to be a local leader. In 1980 he became a member of the Politburo, which made decisions about how the country was governed. In 1990 Gorbachev became the first president of the Soviet Union. He knew big changes were needed.

Gorbachev went to work on restructuring the Soviet government and building stronger relationships with other world leaders. In the late 1980s, he met US President Ronald Reagan for a series of talks to improve international matters and how they were handled. Gorbachev was awarded the Nobel Peace Prize in 1990 for his involvement in the improvement of world development.

Aung San Suu Kyi (1945)

Aung San Suu Kyi was born in 1945 in Myanmar, once known as Burma. Her father led the movement to help free Burma from British control. He was killed when his daughter was only two years old. After her father's death, Suu Kyi lived for many years in the United Kingdom and India. She longed to go back to Myanmar.

When she returned in 1988, the army governed the country. Many people were unhappy with the harsh military rule. Anyone who didn't agree with the government would have been jailed or killed.

Suu Kyi planned rallies and fought for reforms, such as free elections. Her efforts were noticed, and she was put under house arrest in 1989. From her home, Suu Kyi kept on fighting for Myanmar's freedom. She was finally released from house arrest in 2010. In 2015 the first free elections were held in Myanmar. Suu Kyi won a seat in parliament and became state counsellor of Myanmar in 2016.

Fact

Aung San Suu Kyi was given the Nobel Prize for Peace in 1991.

Defining great leadership

Throughout history, famous leaders have been strong and focused. They inspired their followers. Many of them changed the course of history.

Some leaders fought for human rights. Dr Martin Luther King Jr, Aung San Suu Kyi and Mahatma Gandhi fought for the rights of their fellow citizens. To achieve their goals, they often had to put themselves in danger.

Some great leaders have done a lot of harm while protecting their power or land. Julius Caesar and Napoleon Bonaparte started wars, resulting in thousands of deaths. Alexander the Great and Genghis Khan conquered other nations. Many people argue that these people changed the world for the better.

From establishing better trade routes in ancient times to fighting for civil rights in the 1900s, many great leaders had an important impact on the world around them. What do you think?

Glossary

abolish put an end to something officially

activist person who works for social or political change

advocate person who supports a cause

colony place that is settled by people from another country and is controlled by that country

conquest something that is won, such as land, treasure or buildings

diplomat person who represents his or her country's government in a foreign country

discrimination treating people unfairly because of their race, country of birth or gender

invasion when a country's military forces enter another country to take it over

nomadic travelling from place to place in search of food and water

pharaoh king of ancient Egypt

proclamation public announcement or statement

statesman person who helps the government with its decisions and business

suffrage right to vote

traitor someone who aids the enemy of his or her country

treason crime of betraying one's country

Index